THEN & NOW

MEMPHIS

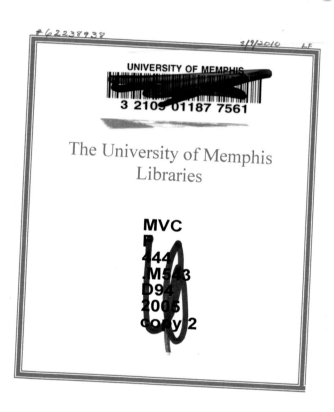

TENNESSEE CLUB, 1907. Built in 1890 as a private club, the Mediterranean-style building is one of preservation's success stories. The building was renovated in 1983 and is today the offices for Burch, Porter and Johnson lawyers.

ON THE COVER: CARNIVORA HOUSE, 1909. The Carnivora House of the Overton Park Zoo was designed by L. M. Weathers in 1909. For many years, it was the lion house, which included Leo, the famous MGM lion seen roaring at the beginning of movies. The building was converted into a restaurant in the 1990s.

Then & Now

MEMPHIS

Robert W. Dye

ARCADIA
PUBLISHING

Published by Arcadia Publishing
Charleston SC, Chicago IL, Portsmouth NH, San Francisco CA

Printed in the United States of America

Library of Congress Catalog Card Number: 2005924399

For all general information contact Arcadia Publishing at:
Telephone 843-853-2070
Fax 843-853-0044
E-mail sales@arcadiapublishing.com
For customer service and orders:
Toll-Free 1-888-313-2665

Visit us on the Internet at www.arcadiapublishing.com

This book is dedicated to my wife, Lisa

MAIN AND MADISON, 1939. The geographic heart of downtown Memphis was the intersection of Main and Madison. Looking toward the southwest, we see the four-story Goodman Building with Lowenstein's just south on Main Street.

CONTENTS

Acknowledgments   6

Introduction   7

1.   Riverfront   9

2.   Cotton Row   15

3.   Downtown Memphis   23

4.   Saturday Night, Sunday Morning   55

5.   Planes, Trains, and Mules   67

6.   Streetscapes   77

7.   Parks   91

ACKNOWLEDGMENTS

The photographs included in this work come from various collections, each one a unique glimpse into the history of Memphis. The Mississippi Valley Collection at the University of Memphis is one of the best photographic archives in the city. I'd like to thank Ed Frank and his staff for their tremendous help. The Shelby County Archives is a most valuable source for information, and their help was greatly appreciated. Photographs were also obtained from the Memphis Room of the Memphis and Shelby County Public Library. Images were also generously loaned from the following individuals and businesses: Hessen Inc., Mary Ann Williamson, MemphisArchives.com, Elmwood Cemetery, Detroit Publishing Company, St. Agnes Academy, Robert William Dye, and the Library of Congress. I would also like to thank those photographers, both known and unknown, who documented the city they called home. It is because of them that we have a better understanding of life in Memphis. They left us literally a snapshot into the history of Memphis.

OVERTON ZOO, 1909. The first animal at the zoo was a small bear named Natch. He was the mascot for the local baseball team until, in 1905, he grew too large to be handled safely. He eventually found his way to Overton Park. Today the zoo is preparing Northwest Passage, a state-of-the-art animal habitat that will include bears, wolves, and seals.

INTRODUCTION

Memphis has changed dramatically from its days as a rowdy river town in the early 1800s to the city of commerce and distribution we have today. Every year, the landscape of the city subtly changes. Sometimes a façade may be added, a roof reconfigured, or a new entrance added. Many times entire buildings—even entire city blocks—are demolished in the name of progress. The urban renewal projects from 1957 to 1977 saw the greatest change to the streetscape of Memphis. Entire neighborhoods were bulldozed. The Pinch district, Beale Street, and the Memphis Medical Center were most affected. Over 560 acres were cleared, demolishing 3,000 structures. The Beale Street project area alone saw over 300 buildings demolished, including the 80-year-old Randolph building at Main and Beale and the Lowe's State Theater on Main Street.

Another reason for the change in appearance is simply modernization. The South Main Historic district was once home to vast cotton warehouses. The area around Fourth and Monroe was once home to numerous livery stables. As the city expanded, the buildings changed owners who modernized them to fit their needs. Today we call it adaptive reuse. Warehouses have become condominiums, fire stations have been turned into museums, and train station lobbies are now banquet halls. But for every success story, there are just as many parking garages, fast food restaurants and vacant lots.

As Memphis grew and residential neighborhoods developed outside the city limits, so did the commercial developments. Laurelwood, Poplar Plaza, and Summer Center were considered on the outskirts of Memphis when they were built. As they drew more and more customers from downtown, businesses such as Goldsmiths, Brys, and Lowensteins began to decline downtown. By the early 1990s, each had closed their doors after being in business on Main Street for more than a century. For many years, people would go downtown to conduct all their business. It was not uncommon for your dentist, lawyer, and accountant to be located in the same building. People would drive from Mississippi and Arkansas to spend the day on Main Street, shopping at Bry's and Goldsmith's, lunching at the Little Tea Room or the Gayoso Hotel, and catching a movie at the Lowe's State or the Warner. It was not uncommon to see chauffeurs standing by their cars on Main Street, waiting to take the wives of cotton planters back to Greenwood or Clarksdale after a day of shopping in Memphis.

For many years Memphis relied on cotton for its lifeblood. The cobblestone landing, Front Street, and Main Street were all paved with cotton. Today new industries, unknown to the cotton factors and steamship captains, have made Memphis the distribution capitol of the world. Medical research, overnight shipping, and tourism have helped to maintain Memphis as one of the great cities of the South. The cobblestones are devoid of the cotton bales of the 1800s. The sounds of the street corner jug bands playing on Beale Street are silent. The grand houses that once lined Vance, Union, and Beale are gone. Of these, all we have left are the images left by photographers, who documented for us a time and place in the history of Memphis.

C AR BARGE, 1949. A river barge brings in the new 1950 models for sale on Union Avenue. For many years, auto row was on Union near Fourth Street.

Chapter 1

RIVERFRONT

MEMPHIS COBBLESTONE LANDING, 1906. The river landing at the bluffs of Memphis were a stopping point for Marquette and Joliet in the 1660s. From that point on, Memphis was a stopping point for anyone going up or down the Mississippi River.

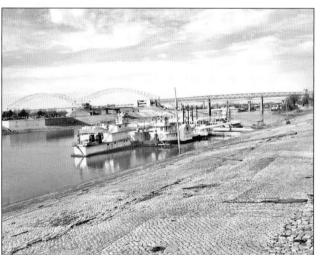

MEMPHIS LEVEE, 1906. The laying of the cobblestone landing began in the 1850s and continued until the late 1880s. The landing was a hub of activity, with cotton being loaded on riverboats on their way to the factories in England and the American Northeast.

MEMPHIS LEVEE, 2005. What to do with the historic cobblestone landing is a source of debate between the preservationists, who wish to preserve its historic value, and the commercial interests, who want to take advantage of its location and marketability.

SKYLINE FROM RIVER, 2005. Today the Custom House and the Cossitt Library still stand but without their towers that were removed long ago during renovations.

SKYLINE FROM RIVER, 1906. For many people in the 19th century, their first view of Memphis was from the river. The imposing twin towers of the Custom House and the tower on the Cossitt Library were a wonderful sight to riverboat passengers.

MEMPHIS **B**LUFFS, **1930.** The area was, for many years, the city dumping ground. Bluff cave-ins were frequent occurrences until the U.S. Army Corps of Engineers stabilized the bluff in the 1930s.

RIVERSIDE **D**RIVE, **1935.** Work began on Riverside Drive in the mid-1930s. The area was graded, and fill was added from dredges in the river.

RIVERSIDE DRIVE, 1937. Built as a joint project with the city and the U.S. Army Corps of Engineers in 1935, Riverside Drive was completed in 1937.

RIVERSIDE DRIVE, 2005. Today Riverside Drive is one of the most scenic streets in Memphis. Tom Lee Park, on the left, was expanded in the 1990s and is the site for the annual Memphis in May Festival. Many fine homes overlook the river from the South Bluffs community, located on the right.

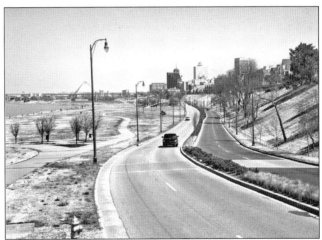

Excursion Boat, 2005. Although the cameras have changed dramatically, people still want to document their boat ride on the Mississippi River.

Excursion Boat, 1915. A young lady photographs her friends on the front of a Memphis excursion boat.

Chapter 2
COTTON ROW

FRONT STREET, 1906. Looking north down Front Street, we see the Cossitt Library and the Custom House. The area between the river and Front Street was set aside by the founders as a public promenade, to be used for the benefit of the citizens and not for business development.

COTTON SIGNS, 1939. Front Street was known as Cotton Row for the numerous cotton merchants located in the area. The Bernstein Cotton Company was located on Union for over 60 years.

FRONT AND UNION, 2005. Today many of the cotton brokers have moved out east with their original buildings being renovated into condominiums, stores, and offices.

FRONT **STREET, 1945.** Front Street was always known for it agricultural businesses: seed and hardware stores, cotton factors, farming supplies, and silo companies. The white building in the center is Union Planters Bank.

FRONT STREET, 2005. Today multistory high-rises have replaced the hardware stores. The tall building on the left is the Morgan Keegan Tower, which replaced the Hotel King Cotton.

FRONT STREET, 1910. On the left are the fire station, Cossitt Library, and the Custom House. On the right is the Reichman–Crosby building, constructed in 1875.

FRONT STREET, 2005. The Shrine Building on the right was constructed in 1923. Built as a source of income and as their headquarters, Al Chymia Shrine Temple occupied the structure until 1936. The building was renovated by Antonio Bologna in 1976 and is today apartments.

CUSTOM HOUSE, 2005. The Custom House has seen several additions: the first in 1903 and then again in 1923. The 1923 addition included paired columns on the east front side based on those from the Louvre in Paris.

CUSTOM HOUSE, 1906. Built in 1876 by architect James G. Hill, the Custom House, with its two large towers, sat high upon the bluff, easily visible to riverboats on the Mississippi.

Cossitt Library, 2005. In 1924, a rear addition was built, and in 1958, the front castle section was demolished and replaced with the modern structure we have today.

Cossitt Library, 1895. Built in 1893, the Cossitt Library was the first public library in Memphis. It was given to the City of Memphis by the daughters of Frederick Cossitt, who had grown up in Memphis but moved on to New York to make a great fortune.

FRONT AND MADISON, 1895. Madison Avenue, like its counterpart in New York, was known for its numerous banks, jewelry stores, and fine restaurants. Banks lined the north side of Madison from Front to Main.

FRONT AND MADISON, 2005. Today the area is seeing a resurgence, with several high-rise apartment buildings and a new Madison Avenue trolley line opening.

FIRE DEPARTMENT, **1910.** Located on Front Street between Union and Monroe, the Reichman-Crosby building was constructed in 1875, and a new front façade was added around 1910. The fire department headquarters were across the street, and the building made a good backdrop for showing off new equipment.

REICHMAN-CROSBY BUILDING, 2005. The building has seen numerous owners and is vacant today.

Chapter 3

DOWNTOWN
MEMPHIS

HOTEL GAYOSO, **1906.** The original Hotel Gayoso was built in 1844 by Robertson Topp, who developed much of the area around Beale and Vance Avenue. The original hotel burned on July 4, 1899, and was replaced by the structure we see above. It last operated as a hotel in 1962, when it was sold to Goldsmith's department store. After renovations in the 1990s, it is today the Gayoso House Apartments.

UNION AVENUE, 1911. This view looking east down Union Avenue toward present-day Danny Thomas Boulevard shows how things looked at the turn of the 20th century. Originally, in the mid-1800s, Union Avenue was the dividing line between Memphis and South Memphis. The bridge covers the Bayou Gayoso, which ran through Beale Street then northward toward the Pinch district.

UNION AVENUE, 2005. Much has changed since 1911; the Bayou Gayoso is now completely underground, the trolley tracks have been removed, and residential homes have been razed for commercial structures.

UNION AVENUE, 1923. Looking west down Union Avenue, we see, on the left, the Tennessee Hotel and the Peabody Hotel. The Tennessee Hotel was built in 1927 and is today a Radison Plaza Hotel. In 1923, the trolley system, with over 300 cars, carried over 30,000 riders daily.

UNION AVENUE, 2005. The Radison Plaza Hotel renovated the Tennessee Hotel in the 1990s, and today it boasts over 280 rooms and suites. The Peabody underwent a major renovation in the 1980s and is regularly listed among the top 100 hotels in the nation.

MAIN STREET, **1895.** Looking north down Main Street during a parade, children climb poles to get a better view as the less adventurous gather at Court Square.

MAIN STREET, 2005. The trolley system, long a mainstay of downtown transportation, was reintroduced in 1993. The trolley line was recently extended out Madison Avenue to the Memphis Medical Center. The first trolleys were introduced on Main Street in 1865 and were mule drawn.

RUSSWOOD PARK, 1925. Memphis's first professional baseball team began in 1901, playing in the area known as Red Elm Bottoms. They changed their name to the Chicks in 1915 and, in 1921, built Russwood Park. The park burned in a tremendous fire in 1960. Today, the site is occupied by the Memphis Medical Center facilities.

RED ELM FIELD, 1915. Red Elm Field was located on Madison just south of Dunlop. Russwood Park was built on this site in 1921.

AUTO ZONE PARK, 2005. After playing for over 40 years at Tim McCarver Stadium located at the fairgrounds, the Memphis Chicks built a new stadium at Fourth and Union. This new stadium has all the amenities of a major league park, with special attention paid to the fans. They also changed their name to the Memphis Redbirds.

COTTON EXCHANGE, 1906. Taken from the same vantage point as "Main Street, 1906" (page 29), this photograph shows Court Square and the Cotton Exchange. To the right of the Exchange is Gaston's Restaurant, founded by John Gaston, who donated money for Gaston Hospital and land for Gaston Park.

EXCHANGE BUILDING, 2005. The 19-story Exchange Building was constructed in 1910 on the site of the Memphis Cotton Exchange. It was the tallest building in Memphis for over 20 years. The office building was renovated in 1995 and is today apartments.

MAIN STREET, 2005. The Kress Block on the west side of Main Street was torn down in the 1920s. For many years, Gerber's department store was located where the Marriot, far right, is located today.

MAIN STREET, 1906. This view, looking south down Main Street, shows many buildings that still stand today, including the D. T. Porter (center), Tennessee Trust (right), and the Commerce Title (behind D. T. Porter).

COTTON EXCHANGE, 1906. Built in 1885 at the corner of Second and Madison, the Memphis Cotton Exchange held the trading floor and offices for the area's powerful cotton merchants. It was demolished in 1910 to make way for the 19-story Exchange Building.

EXCHANGE BUILDING, 2005. The Exchange Building, built in 1910, was, for many years, home to dentists, lawyers, and small businesses. For its first 20 years, it was the tallest building in Memphis, until it was surpassed by the Columbian Mutual tower, now known as the Lincoln American tower. In 1995, the Exchange Building was renovated and is today apartments.

MAIN STREET, 2005. Today Main Street is beginning to become the busy street it once was. Buildings that sat vacant for decades are now being renovated. The Commerce Title, Exchange, and Gayoso buildings have all recently been converted into apartments.

MAIN STREET, 1906. Looking north on Main Street from Union, we see a lone trolley. At its peak, the trolley system carried 30,000 persons a day. On the right is the Memphis Queensware Building, built in 1881 and home for many years to Lemmon and Gale Wholesale Drygoods.

COMMERCE TITLE BUILDING, 1907. Situated on Main Street between Madison and Monroe, the Commerce Title Building was originally known as the Memphis Trust Company Building. The south half of the building was constructed in 1904, with the second half being built 10 years later.

COMMERCE TITLE BUILDING, 2005. Today the Commerce Title Building contains over 150 apartment homes, having been converted from office space in 1998. The building on the right is the William Len, built in 1930. Today it is a Marriot Residence Inn.

MAIN STREET FROM D. T. PORTER, 1910. Here is the view to the north from the roof of the D. T. Porter building, located at Main and Court.

MAIN STREET FROM D. T. PORTER, 2005. Today the view is quite different. The 21-story Lincoln American Building was constructed in 1924 and fashioned after the Woolworth Building in New York.

REX HOTEL, 1954. Located on the north side of Union Avenue, the Rex Hotel was usually overshadowed by the Tennessee Hotel and the Peabody across the street. Damaged by fire in the 1950s, it sat vacant for many years.

AUTO ZONE PARK, 2005. The Rex Hotel was torn down, and today it is the site of Auto Zone Park, the home of the Memphis Redbirds baseball team.

MAIN STREET, 2005. The Orpheum Theater, twice the size of the Hopkins Grand Opera House, opened in 1928. Vaudeville was the main draw in its early years. From 1940 to 1976, it was a first-run movie house. Today it features stage shows and concerts.

MAIN STREET, 1920. The Hopkins Grand Opera House on the left was built in 1890 and burned in 1923; it was replaced with the Orpheum in 1928.

MAIN AT **G**AYOSO, 1910. Looking north down Main Street, we see the Gayoso Hotel on the left, with the Majestic Theater on the right. Beyond the Gayoso is Goldsmith's department store, which was originally located on Beale Street.

MAIN AT **G**AYOSO, 2005. The Gayoso Hotel, left, was purchased by Goldsmiths in the 1960s and most recently converted into the Gayoso House Apartments. The building on the right is The Tower at Peabody Place, a 15-story office building.

MAIN STREET FROM POPLAR, 1915. This view, probably taken from the Overton Hotel, shows the many businesses and shops that once lined Main Street. Crowds had gathered for the arrival of the Liberty Bell, making its way back to Philadelphia from the San Francisco Exposition. The stop at the Poplar Street station drew over 100,000 spectators.

MAIN STREET FROM POPLAR, 2005. Now the area is the site of numerous government buildings, including city hall, the Tennessee State Building, and the Federal Building.

ADAMS AVENUE, 1911. Looking west down Adams Avenue toward Main, we see the newly built police headquarters, fire station, and, in the distance, the Crump Building. Originally the North Memphis Savings Bank, the Crump Building was headquarters of E. H. Crump, Memphis mayor and political powerhouse during the first half of the 20th century.

ADAMS AVENUE, 2005. The police headquarters (right) is undergoing renovation as administrative offices after being closed for over 25 years. Fire Station #3 (center) is today home to the Fire Museum of Memphis, and the Crump Building is home to the chamber of commerce and the Center City Commission.

MADISON AVENUE, 2005. A lone trolley heads toward the medical center. The YMCA, built in 1909 and overlooking the new AutoZone Park, can be seen is the distance.

MADISON AVENUE, 1934. Looking down Madison from Second, we see many of the clothing and jewelry stores in the area. The trolley advertises the new Marlene Dietrich movie, The Scarlet Empress, showing at the Lowes State.

D. T. PORTER BUILDING, 1895. Built by the Continental Bank in 1895, the D. T. Porter Building was the first steel-frame skyscraper in Memphis. At the time of its construction, it was the tallest building in the world to have a circulating hot water heating system.

D. T. PORTER, 2005. The building was renovated in 1983 and is today condominiums. This was one of architect Edward Culliatt Jones's last buildings, and it was placed on the National Register of Historic Places in 1995.

HUNT PHELAN HOME, 2005. Today, the Hunt Phelan home is still owned by the descendents of the original owners, although most of the furnishings and valuable archives were auctioned in 1999. Beale was once lined with many fine homes; sadly the Hunt Phelan residence is the only one left.

HUNT PHELAN HOME, 1865. The Hunt Phelan home, located at Beale and Lauderdale, was built in the early 1840s and served as General Grant's headquarters briefly during the Civil War. The mansion was used as a soldiers' home after the war, lodging over 19,000 persons in 1864 alone.

MADISON AVENUE, 1910. Looking west down Madison toward the Custom House, we see a busy street. Even in 1910, it was hard to find a parking spot. Some things never change.

MADISON AVENUE, 2005. In 2004, trolley service was reintroduced to Madison, running from Front Street to the Memphis Medical Center. The 15-story Tennessee Trust building was converted into The Madison Hotel in 1998.

Titus Block, 1935. Built in 1850 on the corner of Market and Third by Col. Frazer Titus, the apartments were some of the first in Memphis. During the Civil War, Colonel Titus's sister, a well-known Confederate spy, occupied an apartment there.

Uptown Square, 2005. Lauderdale Courts were built in 1936 by the Public Works Administration of Roosevelt's New Deal. The Courts were to provide the poor with decent housing until they could provide for themselves. The area was recently redeveloped as Uptown Square.

MAIN AND BEALE, 1940. The intersection of Main and Beale has changed over time. Jim's Bar and Grill was a popular spot for many years. On the northeast corner was Tony's fruit stand, long an institution in the area. Up the street is Lowes State, where a young Elvis Presley worked as an usher.

MAIN AND BEALE, 2005. Jim's Bar and Grill was torn down to make way for a parking lot for the Orpheum Theater. On the right is the Tri-State Bank.

BEALE STREET, 1920. Known as the birthplace of the blues, Beale Street is recognized worldwide for its musical heritage. Musicians such as Robert Johnson, B. B. King, and Howlin' Wolf have all performed here.

BEALE STREET, 2005. After almost being a victim of urban renewal in the 1970s, Beale Street was reborn in the 1980s and today is one of the major tourist destinations. B. B. King, who once played an amateur contest for a $1 prize, now has his own club at the corner of Beale and Second.

BEALE STREET JUG BAND, 1937. Performing on the corner of Beale and Hernando is one of the famous jug bands. They were called jug bands because one of the musicians usually played a jug. Other instruments included a banjo, guitar, clarinet, and washboard.

PAT O'BRIENS, 2005. For many years, this location was Greeners department store. Today the property is occupied by Pat O'Briens, bringing a little New Orleans to Beale Street.

MARKET HOUSE, 1905. Built in 1899 as a market for a variety of businesses including groceries, dentists, barbers, and shoemakers, the Beale Street Market was one-stop shopping for residents of the famous neighborhood.

HANDY PARK, 2005. The Market House was razed in 1930 to make way for a public park in honor of W. C. Handy. A statue of Handy was added in 1960, and for many years, the park was host to local musicians and jug bands. In 1998, the park was reconfigured with a modern stage and gift shop. Today the sounds of the blues can still be heard echoing down Beale.

PEABODY HOTEL, 1907. Situated on the corner of Main and Monroe, the Peabody was built by Robert Brinkley in 1869 as a wedding present for his daughter. The hotel was named for Brinkley's friend, George Peabody, of New York. The original hotel was enlarged in 1906 and burned in 1923.

BRINKLEY PLAZA, 2005. The Peabody Hotel was rebuilt on Union Avenue in 1924, and the B. Lowenstein and Brothers building was constructed on the site of the old hotel. Lowenstein's went out of business in 1967, and the building was renovated in 1987 and renamed Brinkley Plaza after Robert Brinkley.

BLAKE BUILDING, 2005. The Masonic Lodge was torn down in the early 1900s and replaced with the Germania Bank Building. The Blake Building, constructed in the late 1950s, occupies the site today.

MASONIC LODGE, 1895. After the fall of Nashville during the Civil War, Gov. Isham Harris convened the state legislature on this site in early 1862. The state archives were also briefly stored here.

MADISON AVENUE, 1900. Known as the Wall Street of Memphis for its impressive array of banks, Madison Avenue was the heart of downtown.

MADISON AVENUE, 2005. Today the banks have moved to other locations, being replaced with fitness centers and parking garages.

PEABODY PLACE, 2005. Built in 1998, Peabody Place is the centerpiece of downtown redevelopment. Within walking distance of Beale Street, Auto Zone Park, FedEx Forum, and Gibson guitar factory, the downtown mall attracts tourists and locals with national and local stores.

HULL DOBBS FORD, 1950. Located on Third south of Union, this site was originally a livery stable in the late 1800s. It was the location of the "largest Ford dealership in the world" during the 1950s and 1960s.

ST. AGNES, 1890. St. Agnes Academy was started in 1851 on Vance Avenue. The private girls school is the second oldest in the city. St. Mary's was founded in 1847 as a school for girls at Calvary Episcopal.

ST. AGNES TODAY, 2005. The school moved to its present location on Walnut Grove in 1953, and today it is one of the premier schools in the city.

J. K. PORTER RESIDENCE, 1895. The J. K. Porter Residence was on the southeast corner of Vance and Orleans. The house stood just west of the St. Agnes Academy. Vance Avenue was known for its many fine homes at the turn of the 19th century; now they are but a memory.

VANCE AVENUE MIDDLE SCHOOL, 2005. Vance Avenue Middle School opened in 1971 at the corner of Vance and Orleans. Today it serves more than 550 students in grades six, seven, and eight.

MADISON AT THIRD, 1915.
An early taxi would take
you anywhere for five cents, while
reminding you to "Shop at Brys." The
Cordova Hotel on the right was one
of Memphis's early hotels. Just up the
street was the Southern Bowling Alley.

MADISON AT THIRD, 2005. Today
Third and Madison is quite different.
The large building in the background
is the Exchange Building, constructed
in 1910.

Chapter 4

SATURDAY NIGHT, SUNDAY MORNING

COTTON CARNIVAL, 1955. There was no greater Saturday night than when the Cotton Carnival was in town. A large street carnival was held on Front Street, parades on Main, and dances in all the hotels.

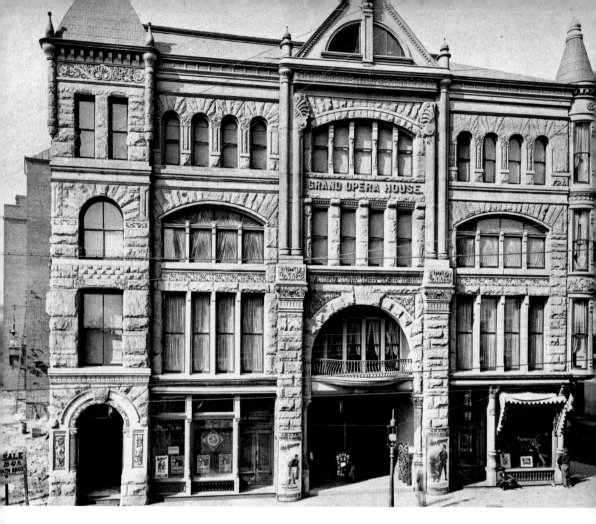

HOPKINS **G**RAND **O**PERA **H**OUSE, **1895.** Built in 1890, the Grand Opera House was known as the finest theater outside of New York. From 1899 until 1923, the theater hosted such stars as Sarah Bernhardt, Lillian Russell, and Harry Houdini. The Grand Opera House burned in 1923.

ORPHEUM **T**HEATER, **2005.** The new theater was rebuilt in 1928 for a cost of $1.6 million and named the Orpheum. For many years, it was a premier movie house in Memphis. In 1984, it was restored to its original grandeur, and today it hosts the best in stage and music.

PARKING CAN BE FUN, 2005.
Today the site of Lowes Palace is a parking garage. Often large parties and concerts are held on its roof.

LOWES PALACE, 1951. Located on Union Avenue between Front and Main, the Lowes Palace was one of the largest movie palaces in Memphis. Elvis Presley worked briefly as an usher just around the corner at the Lowes State theater.

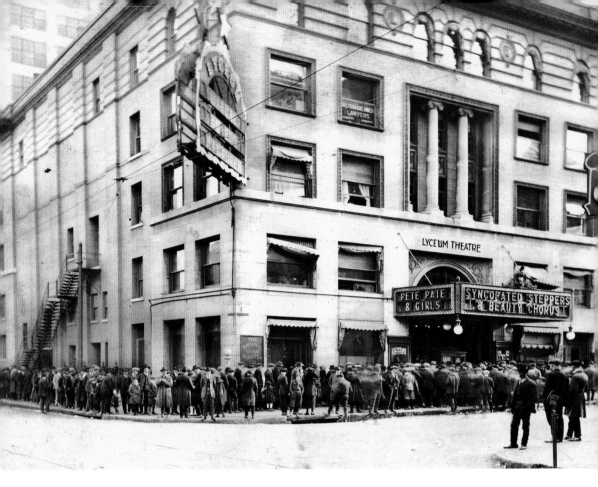

LYCEUM THEATER, 1935. Built in 1894 by H. L. Brinkley, the Lyceum Theater was a legitimate theater until 1919 when it turned to Vaudeville, motion pictures, and boxing. It closed in 1935.

LYCEUM THEATER, 2005. Today the site of the Lyceum Theater is occupied by the Regions Bank Building.

LYRIC THEATER, 2005. Today the site where so many were entertained sits empty. In 1921, the American Legion held a minstrel show there, with a parade led by Mayor Rowlett Paine to advertise the show.

LYRIC THEATER, 1935. Opening in 1908 on Madison, the Lyric was a 1,400-seat musical theater. The best in stage and vaudeville played there, including Sarah Bernhardt and Efram Zimbalist. In its later years, prizefights were held there. The theater burned on January 23, 1941.

OVERTON HOTEL, 1910. Built during the Civil War, it was used as a hospital by both sides. It opened as a hotel on December 5, 1866. The Grand Duke Alexis of Russia spent several nights there in 1872. The hotel was sold to Shelby County in 1874 and used as a courthouse until 1910.

AUDITORIUM AND MARKET HOUSE, 1950. The Auditorium was built in 1924 with public and private money. The name was changed in 1930 to Ellis Auditorium after Robert R. Ellis, a prime motivator in getting the auditorium built. In later years, it was divided into the north and south halls, sharing a stage between them.

ELVIS AT NORTH HALL, 1956.
As a youth, Elvis would sit in
the North Hall and listen to the
Blackwood Brothers and other gospel
groups perform. He first performed at
the North Hall on February 6, 1955.
A year later, he was so popular that
they opened both sides of the large
auditorium to watch him perform.

CANNON CENTER, 2005. In the late
1990s, the Auditorium was demolished,
and in its place, the 2,100-seat Cannon
Center for the Performing Arts was
built. Today it is home to the Memphis
Symphony Orchestra.

WARNER THEATER, 1940. Originally opened as the Pantages Theater at Main and Monroe in 1921, the Warner had two balconies based on Italian Renaissance design. The theater was torn down in 1968 to make way for Commerce Square.

NATIONAL BANK OF COMMERCE, 2005. Designed by Roy Harrover and Associates, the National Bank of Commerce Building was completed in 1970.

St. Mary's Church, 2005. The church first met at this location in 1856, the land being donated by Robert C. Brinkley. At the time, the land was in the suburbs of the city. St. Mary's was the third parish organized in Memphis, with Calvary (1832) and Grace (1853) being mission churches.

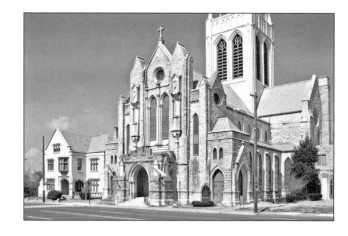

St. Mary's Church, 1912. Located on Poplar near Alabama, the church was the Episcopal Cathedral for the Diocese of Tennessee. Building started in 1895 and was completed in the early 1920s. The Diocesan House to the left of the church, built in 1902, was the residence for the bishop.

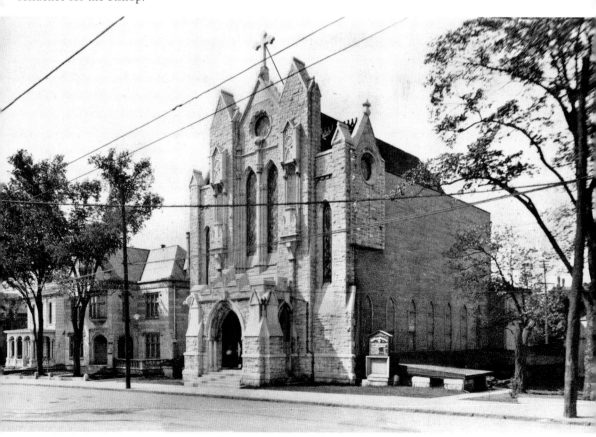

ST. PETER'S CHURCH, 1900. Located on Adams Avenue, St. Peter's Catholic Church was built in 1852 and restored by Antonio Bologna in 1986.

ST. PETER'S CHURCH, 2005. With so many parking garages replacing theaters and fast food restaurants replacing grand mansions, it's nice to see some things have not changed. For over 150 years, St. Peter's Church has welcomed all to the corner of Adams and Third.

FIRST **P**RESBYTERIAN **C**HURCH, **2005.** Today First Presbyterian Church is truly an urban church. Their weekly Sunday soup kitchens feed the needy in downtown Memphis, and the urban ministry programs help families throughout the Greater Mid–South.

FIRST **P**RESBYTERIAN **C**HURCH, **1895.** Built in 1884 by architect Edward Culliatt Jones, the church is located at Poplar and Third. The large steeple was lost in the church's early years and replaced with a square tower. The First Presbyterian Church in Memphis was established in 1828 with five members.

CENTRAL **B**APTIST **C**HURCH, **1890.** Located on Second Street between Beale and Gayoso, this structure literally stood above all others. Built by Edward Culliatt Jones between 1868 and 1885, the church was best known for its 125-foot steeple, the tallest in the city. Memphis had more than 90 churches in or near downtown. Today fewer than 20 are still standing.

PARKING **G**ARAGE, **2005.** The church and its grand steeple were torn down early in the 20th century. The land was used for many years as a filling station and parking lot. The modern multistory parking garage was built for Peabody Place in the late 1990s.

Chapter 5
PLANES, TRAINS, AND MULES

LOUISVILLE AND NASHVILLE (L&N) LOCOMOTIVE #1901, 1914. Memphis has always been a distribution center, from the fur traders who lived here before a city was planned to the world headquarters for FedEx. One of Memphis's nicknames is "America's Distribution Center."

UNION STATION, 1912. Located on Calhoun at Third, Union Station was, to many, the most beautiful station in Memphis. In the 1940s, the grand station had 17 trains arriving daily. It was demolished in 1967.

POSTAL SERVICE BUILDING, 2005. Built in 1970 and designed by Francis Mah and Walk Jones, the United States Automated Handling Facility, as it is formally known, replaced the grand Union Station.

CENTRAL STATION, 2005. Calhoun was renamed in 1994 for Bishop G. E. Patterson, a local pastor. The station was placed on the National Register of Historic Places in 1994.

CENTRAL STATION, 1913. This view is looking east on Calhoun toward Central Station. The station, designed by Daniel Burnham of Chicago, was renovated in 1995 and has been converted into apartments with offices on the ground floor. Amtrak, as it has been known for many years, still has a waiting room for its twice-daily departures.

UNION DEPOT, 1907. Union Depot was located at Main and Calhoun and was the headquarters for several rail lines. The station was demolished in 1912 to make way for the new L&N Central Station.

CENTRAL STATION, 1914. Central Station was the Memphis headquarters for the L&N Railroad. The L&N depot had previously been located in the Poplar Street Station at Front and Poplar.

CENTRAL STATION, 2005.
Today the station looks much
the way it did when it was completed
in 1914. The area surrounding the
station is known as the South Main
Historic district, which includes many
fine restaurants, art galleries, and
antique shops.

**CENTRAL STATION, MAIN WAITING
ROOM, 1914.** Central Station had
as many as 50 trains arriving and
departing daily during its heyday
from 1920 to 1950. The station was
renovated in 1995, with the waiting
room being used today for receptions
and banquets.

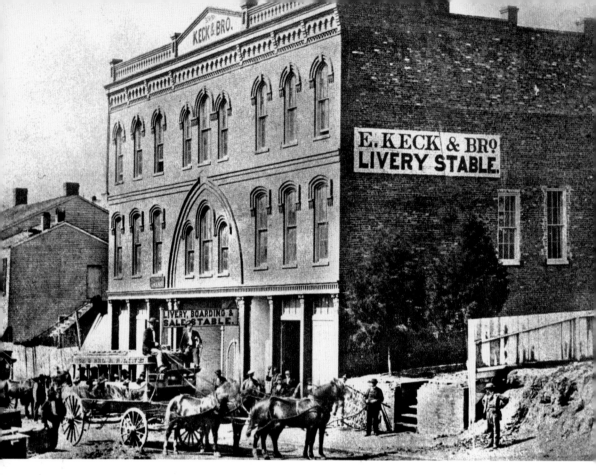

KECK LIVERY STABLE, 1895.
Located on Second between Beale and Gayoso, the Keck Livery Stable was one of many in the city. Memphis once held the distinction as being the world's largest mule market. As many as 60,000 mules were auctioned in a single year. Most were used for farming, although a few had city jobs, pulling the local trolleys or hauling cotton from the riverboats to the warehouses.

GAYOSO AND SECOND, 2005. The area today is occupied by a series of vacant buildings that most recently held Elvis Presley's Memphis, a theme restaurant based on the life and food of the king of rock and roll. The building was also home to Lansky Brothers clothier. Today they are located in the lobby of the Peabody Hotel.

ECHELON APARTMENTS, 2005.
Overlooking Auto Zone Park,
the Echelon apartments provide
downtown living with over 400
apartments, all within walking
distance to many of downtown's
major attractions.

MAMMOTH LIVERY STABLES, 1907.
Located at Fourth and Monroe, the
Mammoth Livery Stables were built
in 1903. It had electric elevators,
and its three stories covered over
79,000 square feet. The building
was decorated for a visit to by Pres.
Theodore Roosevelt.

MEMPHIS AIRPORT, 1929. The city purchased 200 acres for $250,000. Over the next 70 years, the city added onto this, and today the airport covers over 3,330 acres. The original airport handled four flights a day in 1929.

MEMPHIS AIRPORT, 1939. A new terminal building was constructed by the Works Progress Administration in 1939. By this time, the airport was seeing 30 flights a day with such airlines as American, Eastern, and Southern (now Delta).

AIR SHOW, 1929. For the opening of the new airport in 1929, a tremendous air show was produced. Hundreds of the newest airplanes were flown in for the event.

MEMPHIS INTERNATIONAL AIRPORT, 2005. The new airport terminal was built south of the old hangar and tower. The new facility was built in 1959, with additions being completed in 1964.

POPLAR STREET STATION, 1915.
Built in 1896, the station is shown here during a visit of the Liberty Bell in 1915. A parade with over 20,000 marchers celebrated the arrival, and over 100,000 spectators turned out to watch. The station is probably most famous for the fact that Casey Jones left out of it in 1900 for his fateful trip to Vaughn, Mississippi.

FRONT AND POPLAR, 2005. The station was torn down in 1939, and the land has remained vacant ever since. A historical marker now marks the site of the beautiful station.

Chapter 6
STREETSCAPES

THIRD STREET, 1909. Looking down Calhoun from Third Street in 1909, we see a residential district. The road system has changed greatly since then, and the streets have changed names several times.

SECOND AND MILL, 1912. The flood of 1912 was one of the worst on record. The Pinch area, north of downtown Memphis, was the hardest hit. For many, the only way to get around was by boat.

SECOND AND MILL, 2005. Today the area is part of a large revitalization effort in the Pinch district, north of downtown Memphis. The 100-block area is now known as Uptown Memphis and features parks, homes, and businesses just minutes from downtown.

MILL STREET, 2005. New construction and the lure of downtown living have drawn many to live in Greenlaw Place, a new development community in the Pinch district.

MILL STREET, 1912. This view looks east down Mill Street from Second during the flood of 1912. The area was one of the city's first subdivisions, created by William and J. Oliver Greenlaw in 1856. They also built the Greenlaw Opera House at Union and Second.

ELMWOOD CEMETERY, 1880. The cemetery was founded in 1852, with the superintendent's cottage being built in 1866. Politicians, musicians, soldiers, and yellow fever victims lay side by side in one of the most beautiful cemeteries in the South.

ELMWOOD CEMETERY, 2005. The cottage was added onto in 1903 and 1978. In 1978, it was placed on the National Register of Historic Places. Chester Anderson is noted as having the first motorized funeral at Elmwood in June 1911.

VETERANS HOSPITAL, 2005. In the 1930s, the Mallory house was torn down and the Methodist Hospital built on the property. Later, the hospital was sold to the Veterans Administration. Today, the numerous medical buildings are being demolished.

MALLORY RESIDENCE, 1895. William Barton Mallory lived at the corner of Crump Boulevard and Dudley. A veteran of the Civil War, his regiment would camp on his grounds during the reunions held in Memphis. His principal business was the wholesale grocery firm of W. B. Mallory and Sons.

CALHOUN AVENUE, 1914. On the left is Central Station, built in 1914 for the L&N Railroad. Once the station was built, many bars and hotels were established in the area. A watch repair shop was located across the street so conductors could make sure their pocket watches were working correctly.

G. E. PATTERSON AVENUE, 2005. The view has changed little since 1914. On the right is Ernestine and Hazels, a historic bar that has been at that location for many years.

FRONT STREET FROM CENTRAL STATION, 1914. Looking toward Front Street from the roof of Central Station, we see the many houses that once lined the street. The area was primarily residential until the train stations were built at the turn of the 20th century.

FRONT STREET FROM CENTRAL STATION, 2005. From the 1920s to the 1970s, the area around Central Station was a warehouse district. Many of the large cotton warehouses were located in the area. The long vacant buildings are now being converted into apartments and condominiums.

YOUNG AVENUE, 1917. Looking east down Young Avenue from Meda, we see the trolley tracks that took passengers to Montgomery Park, Memphis's finest horse racing track in the late 1800s. The track was located on what is today Libertyland Amusement Park.

YOUNG AVENUE, 2005. The Cooper-Young neighborhood has maintained its eclectic style and distinctive architectural history, becoming one of the most unique neighborhoods, with its diverse restaurants, shops, and galleries.

STONEWALL PLACE, 1924. Looking north down Stonewall from Poplar, we see a row of freshly planted trees. The Memphis Shade Tree Company had just planted many of the trees that still stand today. Stonewall is now in the Evergreen Historic District.

STONEWALL AVENUE, 2005. Originally called Stonewall Place, today Stonewall Avenue is still one of the most beautiful streets in the city. The area is one of the oldest neighborhood associations and also the first historic conservation district in the city. The Evergreen Historic District Association works with other neighborhoods to protect the historic quality of their residential communities.

POPLAR AND EVERGREEN, 1940. Looking east down Poplar from Evergreen, we see the Ritz Theater on the right, with Paris Drugstore on the left.

POPLAR AND EVERGREEN, 2005. Today the area is in the heart of midtown Memphis. The Ritz Theater on the right is now the Circuit Playhouse, showcasing some of the city's best stage talent.

St. Peter's Orphanage, 1910. Built in the late 1890s, St. Peter's Orphanage has helped thousands of children in need over the many years of its service. Located at Poplar and McLean, the 25-acre facility was purchased by Reverend Father Kelly in 1879 and continues to this day to reach out to those who need help.

Target House, 2005. Target House was established to give patients of St. Jude and their families a place to live while receiving treatment for cancer. The facility is one of the bright spots in the city of Memphis.

FORTUNES DRIVE-IN, 1930. The original Fortunes was opened at Union and Somerville in 1920, and in 1922, a second location was added at Union and Belvedere (shown above). Long a hangout for teenagers, the drive-in was one of the first in the nation.

UNION AND BELVEDERE, 2005. Fortunes Drive-In merged with Midwest Dairies in 1937 and maintained a plant at the Union location until the 1980s, when the property was sold to Shell Oil.

CENTRAL HIGH SCHOOL, 2005.
For many years, Central High School was a community school, serving Central Gardens and the growing midtown neighborhoods.

CENTRAL HIGH SCHOOL, 1910.
Central High School was built in 1911 by B. C. Alsup, architect. The school is one of the oldest high-school buildings in the city.

NATIONAL FUNERAL HOME, 1935. Originally a private residence, the National Funeral Home, located on Union between Waldran and Pasedena Place, was the largest funeral service provider in Memphis.

THE BRISTOL ON UNION, 2005. The funeral home was torn down in 2001, and a 220-apartment community was built on its site. This was the funeral home where the body of Elvis Presley was brought to prepare it for burial.

SKATING IN FORREST PARK, 1907. Forrest Park was originally the site of the Memphis Hospital. The statue of Nathan Bedford Forrest was dedicated in May 16, 1905, with over 30,000 people attending the unveiling.

HEBE FOUNTAIN, **1900.** Court Square was one of four original squares laid out in 1819. The other squares are Auction, Market, and Exchange. The fountain was donated by local citizens in 1876 for the centennial of the United States.

HEBE FOUNTAIN, 2005. The Hebe Fountain in Court Square contains, at its top, a reproduction of Antonio Canova's statue of Hebe, cupbearer to the Greek gods. The statue was badly damaged during a storm in 1942.

COURT SQUARE, 1920. This panoramic photograph by J. C. Coovert gives us a 180-degree view of Court Square. Pres. Grover Cleveland addressed a large crowd from the bandstand upon his visit here.

COURT SQUARE, 1930. Court Square has changed little in its 190-year history. It was used for musical concerts in the 1930s and war bond drives during the 1940s, and for many years, children would visit Santa there.

COURT SQUARE, 2005. The park has just seen a complete renovation, with new landscaping and new walkways installed. It is said that Davy Crocket and Sam Houston rested in the park during their visits to Memphis. A small log cabin courthouse was placed here in 1821, but it was used mainly for storage.

JEFFERSON DAVIS PARK, 1915. People gather in the late afternoon to watch a sunset over the Mississippi River.

JEFFERSON DAVIS PARK, 2005. Today the park is still used by those who wish to relax and take it easy.

JEFFERSON DAVIS PARK, 2005. The park looks much like it did when created in 1930. To the north of the park is the new Tennessee State Welcome Center.

JEFFERSON DAVIS PARK, 1937. Jefferson Davis Park became an official park in 1930. For many years, people had used the area to watch the many boats dock at the harbor and to watch the river.

CONFEDERATE PARK, 1910. The site of Confederate Park was a trading post in the late 1700s. During the Civil War, Confederate cannons fired at Northern gunboats on the Mississippi River during the brief Battle of Memphis.

CONFEDERATE PARK, 2005. The park today contains monuments and historical markers dedicated to the Southern cause. A marker for Ginnie Moon tells how she was a Confederate spy and came back after the war to help yellow fever victims.